Connect

SECOND EDITION

Jack C. Richards
Carlos Barbisan

with Chuck Sandy
and Dorothy E. Zemach

Workbook 4

CAMBRIDGE
UNIVERSITY PRESS

University Printing House, Cambridge CB2 8BS, United Kingdom

One Liberty Plaza, 20th Floor, New York, NY 10006, USA

477 Williamstown Road, Port Melbourne, VIC 3207, Australia

314–321, 3rd Floor, Plot 3, Splendor Forum, Jasola District Centre, New Delhi – 110025, India

79 Anson Road, #06–04/06, Singapore 079906

Cambridge University Press is part of the University of Cambridge.

It furthers the University's mission by disseminating knowledge in the pursuit of education, learning and research at the highest international levels of excellence.

www.cambridge.org
Information on this title: www.cambridge.org/9780521737258

First published 2004
Second edition 2010

Printed in Great Britain by Ashford Colour Press Ltd.

A catalog record for this publication is available from the British Library.

ISBN 978-0-521-73721-0 Student's Book 4 (English)
ISBN 978-0-521-73722-7 Student's Book 4 (Portuguese)
ISBN 978-0-521-73725-8 Workbook 4 (English)
ISBN 978-0-521-73726-5 Workbook 4 (Portuguese)
ISBN 978-0-521-73727-2 Teacher's Edition 4 (English)
ISBN 978-0-521-73728-9 Teacher's Edition 4 (Portuguese)
ISBN 978-0-521-73724-1 Class Audio CDs

Art direction, photo research, and layout services: A+ comunicação
Book design: Adventure House, NYC

Table of Contents

Last summer

1 Complete the e-mail message with the correct form of the verbs in the box.

☐ be   ☐ buy   ☐ have   ☐ see   ☐ watch
☐ break   ☑ go   ☐ play   ☐ stay   ☐ write

Hi, Jeff!
    Did you have a good summer vacation? You ___went___ mountain climbing, right? How _____ your trip? Please _____ me a message and tell me.
    I didn't go away this summer. I just _____ home. I _____ a lot of my friends, and we _____ DVDs. One day, while I _____ soccer, I _____ my watch. I _____ a new one the next day.
    I hope you _____ a great vacation. See you at school!
Your friend,
Chris

2 Read the text. Then number the pictures in the correct order.

I'm Kenny Morton. I went to tennis camp with my friends last summer. We got up at 6:00 a.m. every day. That was OK because we also went to bed early. We practiced tennis all the time. At the end of the summer, my best friend, Teddy, was practicing when he fell and broke his arm. That was really too bad. We had a competition on the last day, and I won a prize! After camp was over, I had a lot of summer homework to do. Now I'm back at school.

a. _____   b. _____   c. ___1___   d. _____   e. _____   f. _____

3 Look at the information in Part 2 again. Write questions and answers about Kenny.

1. **Q:** _Where did Kenny go last summer?_   **A:** He went to tennis camp.

2. **Q:** Who did he go with? **A:** _____

3. **Q:** Were they practicing tennis all day? **A:** _____

4. **Q:** What time did they get up? **A:** _____

5. **Q:** _____   **A:** No, they didn't. They went to bed early.

6. **Q:** _____   **A:** He broke his arm.

Lesson 2 A new school year

1 Match the words to make verb phrases. Then write the verb phrases.

1. start _e_   a. tennis   _start a CD collection_
2. join ____   b. karate   _____
3. play ____   c. good grades   _____
4. get ____   d. a computer course _____
5. do ____   e. a CD collection   _____
6. take ____   f. the art club   _____

2 Complete the conversations with the correct form of *would like to,* *want to,* *be going to,* or *have to.*

1. A Would you like to join the chess club?

   B Yes. _I'd like to_ join the chess club. It sounds like fun!

2. A Do your sisters have to take a math class this year?

   B Yes, they do. _____ take math every year.

3. A Does Alberto have to study hard this year?

   B Yes. _____ study really hard! His parents want him to get better grades.

4. A Are they going to see the play today?

   B No, they're not. _____ see the play tomorrow.

5. A Would your brother like to learn to speak German?

   B Yes. _____ learn German. It's a beautiful language.

6. A Do you want to visit the U.S. next year?

   B Yes, I do. _____ visit Los Angeles and Seattle.

3 Write sentences with your own information. Use the verb phrases in Part 1 and *would like to* or *want to* for hopes and wishes, *be going to* for definite plans, and *have to* for obligations.

1. _I'd like to start a CD collection._
2. _____
3. _____
4. _____
5. _____
6. _____

Mini-review

1 **Write sentences about hopes and wishes, obligations, or definite plans.**

1. **hope:** my best friend / join a new club
   My best friend wants to join a new club.
   OR *My best friend would like to join a new club.*

2. **wish:** Juanita / take piano lessons

   _____

3. **hope:** my parents / take a trip this weekend

   _____

4. **definite plan:** Jorge and Jessica / go out tonight

   _____

5. **obligation:** Carlos / get good grades this year

   _____

6. **definite plan:** my friends and I / go camping

   _____

7. **obligation:** you / get up early tomorrow

   _____

8. **wish:** Laura / stay out late tonight

   _____

9. **hope:** Keiko and Yuko / travel to Canada next year

   _____

10. **definite plan:** I / go to the movies on Saturday

    _____

2 **Answer the questions with your own information.**

1. What were you doing last Saturday at 10:00 a.m.? _____

2. What would you like to do tomorrow? _____

3. What were you doing last night at 7:00 p.m.? _____

4. What did you do last Saturday night? _____

5. What would you like to do in English class? _____

6. What subjects do you have to study next year? _____

7. What do you want to do in five years? _____

8. What are you going to do tomorrow? _____

Life events

1 **Write sentences in the simple past.**

1. Kenji / live in Argentina / learn Spanish

   When _Kenji lived in Argentina, he learned Spanish_____.

2. Maria / make new friends / join the tennis team

   _____ when _____.

3. Kim and Cody / learn to dance / take dance lessons

   _____ when _____.

4. Nina / fall off her horse / break her arm

   When _____.

5. Paulo / go camping / lose his hat

   When _____.

6. I / get a cell phone / start high school

   _____ when _____.

2 **Look at the time line below. Then write sentences about the events in Andy's life.**

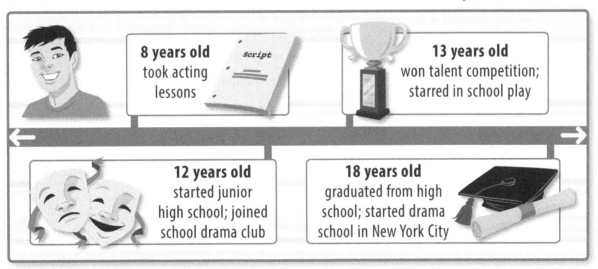

8 years old
took acting lessons   *script*

13 years old
won talent competition;
starred in school play

12 years old
started junior
high school; joined
school drama club

18 years old
graduated from high
school; started drama
school in New York City

1. _When Andy was eight, he took acting lessons._ OR _Andy took acting lessons when he_

   _was eight_____.

2. _____

3. _____

4. _____

5. _____

6. _____

7. _____

Then and now

1 Write sentences with *used to* and *not anymore.*

1. (Aria / shy) *Aria used to be shy, but she isn't anymore.*

2. (I / like this song) _____

3. (Sandra / play the piano) _____

4. (I / take math) _____

5. (you / play computer games) _____

6. (Bill / stay up late) _____

7. (Keith and Marco / wear glasses) _____

8. (I / drink soda) _____

2 Look at the information about Marissa's life. Then write sentences about how her life has changed.

Before high school	Now
took easy classes	takes difficult classes
had lots of free time after school	has no free time
knew just a few people	knows many people
had a CD player	has an MP3 player
listened to country music	listens to rock music
read comic books	reads mystery stories
stayed home on the weekend	goes camping on the weekend

1. *She used to take easy classes, but she doesn't anymore. Now she takes difficult classes.*

2. _____

3. _____

4. _____

5. _____

6. _____

7. _____

1 **Read the article quickly. What's the name of Jason's online store?**

_____

Pencil Bugs

When Juliet Olsen was only nine years old, she started to make colored rubber-band bracelets to go with her favorite clothes. She called them Candy Bands, and she decided to sell them. Juliet and her parents started making the Candy Bands, and Juliet's mother created a Web site for the business. The Candy Bands are all different. Each one has a different pattern.

When Juliet was 12, people were still buying Candy Bands. Juliet wanted to sell more things, so she opened an online store called Candy Bands Shop. Now people from all over the U.S. can buy earrings, necklaces, rings, hair bands, and many other accessories. Luckily for Juliet and her family, the business is doing very well. Candy Bands bracelets are still the best-loved items.

Juliet would like to write books and create videos about how to make rubber-band jewelry. She also wants to create a Candy Bands video game. Juliet tells others, "Give your idea a try. You never know what might happen."

2 **Complete the sentences with the words in the box.**

☐ all over   ☐ best-loved   ☑ decided   ☐ happen   ☐ luckily

1. I ___decided___ to get new shoes with the money I got for my birthday.

2. I'd like to travel _____ South America and make friends in every country.

3. I was late for class yesterday, but _____ the teacher was late, too!

4. This book is very exciting. You never know what's going to _____ next.

5. Mozart wrote some of the _____ music in the world.

3 **Read the article in Part 1 slowly. Answer the questions.**

1. How old was Jason when he started his business? _He was nine years old._

2. What are Pencil Bugs? _____

3. Who created the Web site for the Pencil Bugs? _____

4. What can people buy in the Pencil Bugs online store? _____

5. What's one plan Jason has for the future? _____

Unit 1 Check Yourself

1 **Complete the sentences with the simple past or the past continuous.**

1. We _were walking_ (walk) in the park when we ___met___ (meet) some friends.
2. When he _____ (be) a child, Martin _____ (take) piano lessons.
3. When it _____ (start) to rain, the children _____ (play) outside.
4. I _____ (think) about you when you _____ (call).
5. Kelly _____ (break) her arm when she _____ (play) volleyball.
6. When I _____ (be) five years old, I _____ (start) school.

2 **How did Greenville change? Look at the information. Then write sentences.**

Greenville in 1956

Greenville now

☑ small town / city   ☐ had a lot of bicycles / has a lot of cars

☐ quiet / noisy   ☐ had a lot of trees / has a shopping mall

1. _Greenville used to be a small town, but it isn't anymore. Now it's a city._
2. _____
3. _____
4. _____

3 **Write sentences about hopes and wishes, obligations, or definite plans.**

1. Liz / work in a bookstore / next summer

   definite plan: _Liz is going to work in a bookstore next summer._

2. I / do English and math homework / tonight

   obligation: _____

3. we / join a new club / in September

   hope: _____

4. my classmates / go to college / next year

   definite plan: _____

5. Jorge / play soccer in the park / this weekend

   wish: _____

8   Check Yourself

Lesson 5 · Predictions

1 Cara was born in April. Read the predictions for this year for people born in April. Then answer the questions.

Were you born in April? You won't have much money this year, so you won't buy too many things! You'll take a few short trips this year, but you won't take a long trip. You'll have a fight with your best friend in May. Dont worry — you'll be friends again in June!

1. Will she have a lot of money this year? *No, she won't.*

2. Will Cara buy a lot of things? _____

3. Will she take any short trips this year? _____

4. Will she take any long trips this year? _____

5. Will she have a fight with a friend? _____

2 Write questions with the verb phrases in the box.

☐ buy the shirt ☐ cook dinner ☑ miss the bus
☐ catch the ball ☐ go to the library ☐ see a movie

1. **Q:** *Will they miss the bus?*
   A: No, they won't.

2. **Q:** _____
   A: Yes, he will.

3. **Q:** _____
   A: Yes, they will.

4. **Q:** _____
   A: No, he won't.

5. **Q:** _____
   A: No, I won't.

6. **Q:** _____
   A: Yes, she will.

3 Toshi is thinking about the future. Write sentences about his predictions. Use *will* or *won't*.

1. (animals / talk) *Animals will talk.*

2. (people / not get sick) _____

3. (people / go on vacations in outer space) _____

4. (men / not wear ties) _____

When I'm older

1 **Complete the conversation with the sentences in the box.**

> ☐ No. She probably won't go to college until next year.
> ☐ No. She probably won't go to Europe.
> ☐ No, she won't. She'll probably travel with her friends.
> ☑ She'll probably take a trip.
> ☐ She'll probably work for our father in his office.
> ☐ She probably will.
> ☐ She probably won't.

Kim Your sister's graduating from high school this year, right? What's she going to do?

Greg I'm not sure. *She'll probably take a trip.* She wants to relax after she graduates.

Kim Where will she go? Europe?

Greg _____ She doesn't have a lot of money.

Kim Will she travel alone?

Greg _____

Kim And after that? Will she go to college?

Greg _____ She needs to earn some money before she goes to college.

Kim So, what will she do this year?

Greg _____ He needs help.

Kim Maybe someday she'll get a great job!

Greg _____ She's smart. But she'll have to finish college first.

Kim If she lives at home for another year, she can help you with your Spanish homework.

Greg _____ She says I have to learn Spanish by myself.

Kim Then we can work together. I have to study Spanish this year, too!

2 **Make verb phrases with the words below and *be*, *get*, and *go*.**
Then make predictions about yourself. Use *will probably* or *probably won't*.

1. famous   *be famous*   *I probably won't be famous.*
2. a driver's license   _____   _____
3. to college   _____   _____
4. rich   _____   _____
5. a job   _____   _____
6. an actor   _____   _____
7. a pet   _____   _____
8. married   _____   _____

Mini-review

1 Complete the text with *want to*, *will*, or *won't*.

I _want to_ travel to South America. I probably
_____ visit all the countries, but I _____
definitely visit most of them. I'd like to go
camping most of the time, so I probably
_____ visit a lot of cities. I _____ see the
rain forest, so I _____ go hiking through
the jungle or take a boat trip. I _____
probably see a lot of animals. I _____ bring
my camera, but I probably _____ take very
good pictures. I'm a terrible photographer!

2 Complete the questions. Use *Will*, the words in the box, and the cues. Then write
answers with *will*, *won't*, *will probably*, or *probably won't* and your own information.

☐ buy ☐ get ☑ give ☐ go to ☐ record ☐ take ☐ travel to

1. your math teacher / the class a test this week

   Q: _Will your math teacher give the class a test this week?_
   A: _No, she probably won't._

2. you / a job this summer

   Q: _____
   A: _____

3. your favorite singer / some new songs this year

   Q: _____
   A: _____

4. you / bed early tonight

   Q: _____
   A: _____

5. you / a new computer next month

   Q: _____
   A: _____

6. your best friend / Venezuela this fall

   Q: _____
   A: _____

7. your family / a vacation this year

   Q: _____
   A: _____

Teen Center

1 Complete the crossword puzzle with the words in the box.

☐ activity ☐ edit ☐ learn ☐ racket
☐ articles ☑ join ☐ martial ☐ take

Across

2. This year I'm going to _join_ the photography club.

6. A reporter writes _____ for the newspaper.

8. After you make your music video, you might need to _____ it.

Down

1. Ballroom dancing is my favorite after-school _____ .

3. To learn salsa, _____ a dance class!

4. Join the _____ club and play tennis.

5. Karate is a type of _____ art.

7. Do you want to _____ how to make a scrapbook?

2 Write sentences with *might* or *might not*.

1. Kelly loves to draw, but she's very busy this semester.
   (an art class) _She might not take an art class this semester._

2. Sam and Max like to try new foods.
   (cooking class) _____

3. Jason and I aren't good writers.
   (reporters) _____

4. I play the drums.
   (marching band) _____

5. Karen doesn't like dancing.
   (a dance class) _____

6. Sheila isn't good at badminton.
   (racket club) _____

7. John and Dave watch a lot of karate movies.
   (a martial arts class) _____

8. We take a lot of good photos.
   (make a scrapbook) _____

After high school

1 Look at Serena's and Dennis's plans for the future. Then write sentences with *be going to*, *will*, *will probably*, *probably won't*, or *might*.

> ✓ = a definite plan   **o** = a probable plan   **?** = a possible plan

Serena

- **o** visit my grandparents
- ✓ find an apartment in the city
- ✓ go to college
- **o** not take violin lessons
- **?** take a dance class

Dennis

- **?** take a computer class
- ✓ get a job
- **o** take a vacation
- **o** not go on a group tour
- **?** travel alone

1. *She'll probably visit her grandparents.*
2. _____
3. _____
4. _____
5. _____

6. _____
7. _____
8. _____
9. _____
10. _____

2 Write sentences about your future plans and the plans of people you know.

1. **definite plan:** my family
   My family will travel to Puerto Rico this summer.
   OR *My family is going to travel to Puerto Rico this summer.*

2. **probable plan:** my friend
   _____

3. **possible plan:** my English teacher
   _____

4. **probable plan:** my classmates
   _____

5. **definite plan:** I
   _____

6. **possible plan:** my favorite sports team
   _____

1 **Read the article quickly. Will tests in the future be the same as tests today?**

Schools of the Future
by Richard Morton

Some people predict that schools in the future will be different from schools today. How will they be different? First, they'll be smaller. Many schools will have only about 100 students.

Second, schools probably won't have different grades — students of different ages will be in the same grade. Students will also choose the subjects they want to study, and they'll work together on projects. They'll use computers to work with students around the world. Students will create virtual cities and countries and solve problems in them. They will study a lot of languages, too.

Tests will be very different, too. To pass them, students won't only answer questions — they will have to do other things. For a science test, a student might have to make a robot. For a history test, a student might create a museum exhibit. A language arts test might give students a headline, and ask them to write an article about it on the computer.

Schools in the future won't be easier than schools today, but one thing is certain: They will be more exciting!

2 **Complete the sentences with the words in the box.**

| ☐ ages | ☐ certain | ☐ headline | ☐ predict | ☑ virtual |

1. With a computer, you can go on a _virtual_ tour of London.

2. Exercise is good for people of all _____ . Children, teens, and adults all need it.

3. When I saw the name of our school in a front-page _____ , I bought the newspaper.

4. Do you believe people can _____ the future?

5. I wasn't _____ about the answer to that test question, but I knew the others.

3 **Read the article in Part 1 slowly. What does Richard Morton predict about schools of the future? Write *T* (True) or *F* (False). Then correct the false statements.**

1. Morton believes that schools in the future will be ~~bigger~~. _F_   *smaller*

2. Students of different ages will be in the same grade. _____

3. Students will use computers to work with teachers around the world. _____

4. Students won't only answer questions to pass tests in the future. _____

5. Schools will be more boring than schools today. _____

1 Look at the predictions about cars in the future. Then write sentences.

Cars in the Future

✗ use gas ✓ be small ✓ fly in the sky ✓ go very fast ✗ have wheels

✓ = will happen
✗ = won't happen

1. _Cars won't use gas._
2. _____
3. _____
4. _____
5. _____

2 Complete the conversations. Write sentences with *will, won't, might,* or *might not.*

1. **A** Are you feeling OK?

   B No, I'm not. I feel awful. (go to school today) _I won't go to school today._

2. **A** Are your neighbors going on vacation?

   B They're not sure. (go to Costa Rica) _____

3. **A** Are you going to go to the mall with us this afternoon?

   B I don't know. I'm a little tired. (not go with you) _____

4. **A** Will you walk to the park?

   B No, I won't. It's very far away. (ride my bike) _____

5. **A** What will you do your report on?

   B I like Magellan and I know a lot about him.

   (write about him) _____

6. **A** Are you going to join the talent show?

   B Yes, I am, but I'm not sure what I'll do. (play the guitar or sing) _____

3 Answer the questions.

1. Will Evan watch TV tonight? (no / probably) _No. He probably won't watch TV tonight._
2. Is Amy going to the concert? (yes) _____
3. Will your parents drive you to my house? (yes / probably) _____
4. Will you do your homework on Friday night? (no) _____
5. Will it rain tomorrow? (no / probably) _____
6. Will you go to college? (yes) _____
7. Will Carl buy a CD today? (yes / might) _____
8. Are your parents going to go to Rio next year? (no) _____

Weekend plans

1 Complete the conversations. Accept or refuse the invitations.

1. **A** Would you like to play tennis with me?

   B *Sure, I'd love to.* I'll get my racket!

2. **A** Would you like to go to the park on Saturday?

   B _____ I'm going to my cousin's house on Saturday.

3. **A** Would you like to go swimming with me this afternoon?

   B _____ I have to go to soccer practice.

4. **A** Would you like to go to a movie this weekend?

   B _____ Let's see a comedy!

5. **A** Would you like to come over this weekend?

   B _____ I'm going camping with my family.

6. **A** Would you like to take a dance class with me?

   B _____ How about a ballroom-dancing class?

2 Write invitations with *Would you like to.*

1. watch *Star Wars*

   Q: *Would you like to watch Star Wars?*

   A: Sure, I'd love to. *Star Wars* is one of my favorite movies.

2. go skiing on Saturday

   Q: _____

   A: I'm sorry, but I can't. I don't know how to ski!

3. go to the circus

   Q: _____

   A: Yes, I'd love to. I really like the circus.

4. drive go-carts

   Q: _____

   A: Sure, I'd like to. We can race each other!

5. play soccer this weekend

   Q: _____

   A: I'm sorry, but I can't. Can we play next weekend?

6. have lunch

   Q: _____

   A: I'd love to, but I can't. I have a chess club meeting at lunchtime.

Evening plans

1 Complete the conversations with the sentences in the box.

☐ Absolutely not! You can't drive.
☐ No, I'm sorry. My back hurts.
☐ No, I'm sorry. I'll be home late.
☐ Sure. But please be careful with it.
☐ Sure. I'll call you at 7:00.
☑ Yes, of course. I'm good at history.

1. **A** Could you help me with my homework?

   B *Yes, of course. I'm good at history.*

2. **A** Could you help me move this table?

   B _____

3. **A** Can I try your digital camera?

   B _____

4. **A** Can I borrow your car tonight, Dad?

   B _____

5. **A** Can I come over after school?

   B _____

6. **A** Could you call me later?

   B _____

2 Write questions to ask for permission or to make a request.

1. (I / use / your eraser) *Can I use your eraser?*
2. (you / explain / this math problem) _____
3. (I / borrow / money for lunch) _____
4. (you / open / the window) _____

3 Answer the questions in Part 2.

1. (yes) *Yes, of course. / Sure.*
2. (yes) _____
3. (yes) _____
4. (no) _____

Mini-review

1 **Complete the conversations with *can*, *could*, or *would*.**

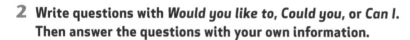

1. **A** Hey, _would_ you like to borrow this magazine?

   B I have to get to class. _____ I borrow it later?

2. **A** _____ I use your new game?

   B Yes. It's a lot of fun. You'll enjoy it.

3. **A** _____ you help me find information for my report?

   B Yes, of course. _____ you like to meet tonight?

4. **A** _____ you like to go to a movie tonight?

   B Sure, but _____ you lend me some money? I don't have any!

5. **A** _____ I go to Dave's party this weekend, Mom?

   B Yes, all right. But _____ you clean your room first?

6. **A** Hi, Fran. _____ you like to do something with me this weekend?

   B Sure, I'd like to. _____ you call me after school? We can make plans then.

2 **Write questions with *Would you like to*, *Could you*, or *Can I*.**
   Then answer the questions with your own information.

1. you / going camping

   Q: _Would you like to go camping?_
   A: _____

2. you / lend / your notebook

   Q: _____
   A: _____

3. you / explore / a rain forest

   Q: _____
   A: _____

4. I / stay out late / tonight

   Q: _____
   A: _____

5. you / clean / the cafeteria

   Q: _____
   A: _____

6. I / borrow / your cell phone

   Q: _____
   A: _____

Making plans

1 Complete the sentences with the clauses in the box.

> ☐ Danny might lend you some money
> ☑ he'll probably help make dinner
> ☐ I might ask him to help me with my homework
> ☐ I won't watch that horror movie
> ☐ my family will probably move
> ☐ my friends might have a barbecue
> ☐ she'll probably miss the show
> ☐ we'll take the bus

1. If my father comes home early, *he'll probably help make dinner* _____ .

2. _____ if it's too scary.

3. If the weather is nice this weekend, _____ .

4. _____ if you ask him.

5. If Giovanni is finished with his homework, _____ .

6. _____ if we find a larger house.

7. If Carla is late, _____ .

8. _____ if we go downtown.

2 Answer the questions in two different ways. Use *if* and your own information.

1. What will you do after school today?
   will: (tired / not tired) *If I'm tired, I'll sleep. If I'm not tired,*
   I'll play baseball.

2. What movie will you see?
   might: (see a comedy / see an action movie) _____

3. What will you do tonight?
   will probably: (have homework / don't have homework) _____

4. What will you do this weekend?
   won't: (rainy / cloudy) _____

5. What will you buy at your favorite store?
   might: (a lot of money / a little money) _____

6. What will you eat for lunch today?
   will: (very hungry / not very hungry) _____

Lesson 12 · Vacation plans

1 Complete these instructions for using a new computer printer with *before*, *while*, and *after*.

1. Read the instructions *before* you take the printer out of the box.

2. _____ you take the printer out of the box, put it on the table.

3. _____ you turn on the computer, connect it to the printer.

4. Turn on the printer _____ you turn on the computer.

5. Make sure you add paper _____ you try to print!

6. And remenber – never eat or drink _____ you are near your printer.

2 Write sentences.

1. Ali / going to go swimming / finish / his homework
   (after) *Ali is going to go swimming after he finishes his homework.*

2. you / should close the door / come in
   (after) _____

3. I / going to study Italian / be / in Rome
   (while) _____

4. Gino and Marie / have to study / take the big test
   (before) _____

3 Write sentences with your own information.

1. (before I go to bed) *Before I go to bed, I might read a book.* OR *I might read a book before I go to bed.*

2. (after I finish this workbook page) _____

3. (while I'm in school next week) _____

4. (after I finish high school) _____

1 **Read the blog quickly. Check (✓) the correct ending to the statement.**

You should ask your parents for permission when they're:

☐ asking you questions.   ☐ not busy.   ☐ doing chores.

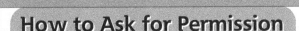
www.ask4permission.gc

How to Ask for Permission

There's a big party tomorrow night. You made fuzzy plans to go with your friends, but you need your parents' permission before you can make firm plans. How do you ask for permission? Here's some advice:

1. Before you ask, do your homework and your chores. If you don't, your parents might tell you to stay home and finish them.

2. Choose a convenient time to ask them. Don't ask them when they're busy.

3. When you ask for permission, be sure to say please.

4. Expect some questions from them. They'll probably ask things like "Where's the party?" "How are you going to get there?" "What time will you get home?" Have your answers ready.

5. Finally, if they say no, try to understand. Remember, if your parents say no, it's probably because they want you to stay safe.

2 **Complete the sentences with the words in the box.**

☐ convenient   ☑ expect   ☐ firm   ☐ fuzzy   ☐ permission

1. I didn't ___expect___ a birthday present from my friends. It was a great surprise.

2. I'm not sure I can go to the movies next weekend, but let's make _____ plans to go.

3. I never go out without my parents' _____ .

4. What's a _____ time to meet to talk about our science project?

5. I know my cousin will join us soon. Our plans were _____ . He's just late.

3 **Read the blog in Part 1 slowly. Circle the correct words to complete the sentences.**

1. You should do your chores (after / before) you ask for permission.

2. You should choose a (convenient / calm) time to ask your parents for permission.

3. It's important to say (you want to go / please).

4. When you ask for permission, your parents (will probably / probably won't) ask some questions.

5. If your parents say no, you should (understand / ask again later).

1 Write questions. Then write acceptances or refusals.

1. **invitation:** play tennis with me today
   Q: *Would you like to play tennis with me today?*
   A: refuse: *I'm sorry, but I can't. I hurt my arm.*

2. **request:** lend me $10
   Q: _____
   A: refuse: _____

3. **permission:** stay out late tonight
   Q: _____
   A: accept: _____

4. **invitation:** come over tonight
   Q: _____
   A: accept: _____

2 Complete the cues with the words in the box. Then write sentences with *if*.

☑ go skiing   ☐ go to sleep   ☐ go to the beach   ☐ not eat lunch

1. it snows / *go skiing*
   (probably) *If it snows, I'll probably go skiing.*

2. it's sunny / _____
   (might) _____

3. I'm not hungry / _____
   (won't) _____

4. I'm exhausted / _____
   (probably) _____

3 Read Jay's notes about his ski vacation. Then write sentences with *before*, *while*, or *after*.

> First, I'm going to find my skis. I think they're in the garage. Then I have to buy new gloves and a new hat. I can buy them at the same time. On vacation, I'm going to take skiing lessons. I'm going to make friends with the other kids who are taking lessons. When I get back, I have to write a report for school.

1. find his skis / go on vacation *He's going to find his skis before he goes on vacation.*
2. buy new gloves / buy a hat _____
3. take skiing lessons / find his skis _____
4. make new friends / take skiing lessons _____
5. write a report for school / get home _____

Teens online

1 **Complete the answers with the gerund form of the verb phrases in the box.**

> ☐ (Chat) online is one of my favorite activities.   ☐ (Listen) to music is great!
> ☐ (Find) information online takes a long time.   ☑ (Play) computer games is boring.
> ☐ (Go) to the beach is nice when it's hot.   ☐ (Play) racket sports isn't fun for me.

1. **Q:** Do you like computer games?   **A:** No, I don't. *Playing computer games is boring.*

2. **Q:** Do you like music?   **A:** Yes, I do. _____

3. **Q:** Do you play racket sports?   **A:** No, I don't. _____

4. **Q:** Do you go to the beach in the summer?   **A:** Yes, I do. _____

5. **Q:** Do you chat online?   **A:** Yes, I do. _____

6. **Q:** Do you find information online?   **A:** No, I don't. _____

2 **Answer the questions in Part 1 with your own information.**

1. _____
2. _____
3. _____
4. _____
5. _____
6. _____

3 **Write answers. Use short answers and gerunds as objects.**

1. **Q:** Does Wendy like to ski?

   A: (yes) *Yes, she does. She likes skiing.* _____

2. **Q:** Does Paul like to dance?

   A: (no) _____

3. **Q:** Do your parents like to use e-mail?

   A: (yes) _____

4. **Q:** Does Ms. Hill like to do crossword puzzles?

   A: (yes) _____

5. **Q:** Do your sisters like to do chores?

   A: (no) _____

6. **Q:** Does your father like to play video games?

   A: (no) _____

7. **Q:** Do your friends like to go to the movies?

   A: (yes) _____

UNIT 4 People

Personality types

1 Complete the puzzle. Then write the mystery word for a popular
personality type.

> ☐ bad-tempered ☑ forgetful ☐ independent ☐ thoughtful
> ☐ creative ☐ hardworking ☐ organized ☐ trustworthy

Clues

1. Someone who doesn't remember things is _____ .
2. A _____ person might be good at art or music.
3. If the things in your room aren't in order, you should be more _____ !
4. Don't get angry too often. No one likes a _____ friend!
5. Someone who is _____ does a lot of things without help.
6. Students who are _____ often get good grades.
7. A _____ person does nice things for friends.
8. Your parents want you to be _____ and honest.

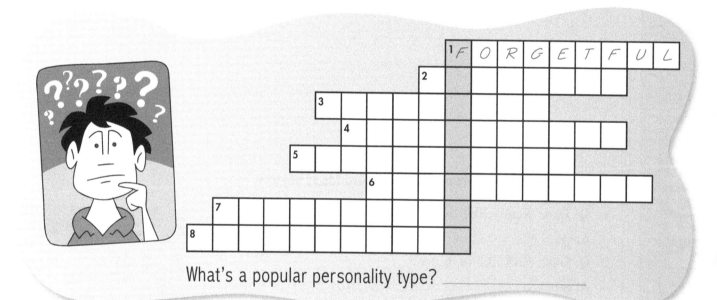

What's a popular personality type? _____

2 How are these people similar? Write sentences.

1. Sebastian is outgoing. (Mei Mei and Tamia) *Mei Mei and Tamia are, too.*
2. Carrie is creative. (her brother) _____
3. My mother doesn't want help doing things. (my father) _____
4. I'm not athletic. (my cousins) _____
5. Kenji studies hard. (Aya and Miho) _____
6. Sue doesn't like going out alone. (her friends) _____
7. I make friends easily. (my sister) _____
8. Selma isn't forgetful. (Wayne) _____

Mini-review

1 **Complete the questions with gerunds as objects.**

1. **Q:** Do you like *doing crossword puzzles* ?
   A: Yes, I do. Crossword puzzles are great!

2. **Q:** Do you like _____ ?
   A: No, I don't. I can't swim, and I don't know how to surf or water-ski.

3. **Q:** Do you enjoy _____ ?
   A: No, I don't. I don't know how to play chess!

4. **Q:** Do you like _____ ?
   A: Yes, I do. I go to the library every week.

5. **Q:** Do you enjoy _____ ?
   A: No, I don't. But my parents always have a lot of things for me to do, like washing the dishes.

6. **Q:** Do you enjoy _____ ?
   A: Yes, I do. My friends play games online, too.

2 **Read Walter's information. Write about his likes, dislikes, and personality. Then write sentences agreeing with Walter's preferences and personality.**

> Likes: do karate, babysit   Personality: be thoughtful, be outgoing
> Dislikes: play baseball, listen to classical music

1. *Walter likes doing karate.*   *I do, too. Doing karate is fun!*
2. _____   _____
3. _____   _____
4. _____   _____
5. _____   _____
6. _____   _____

Unusual people

1 **Write sentences about the people.**

1. have / history teacher / collect cars

I have a history teacher
who collects cars.

2. know / brother and sister / surf in competitions

_____

_____

3. met / swimmer / be an Olympic champion

_____

_____

4. met / teen / collect spiders

_____

_____

5. have / friend / be good at English

_____

_____

6. know / woman / go camping in the snow

_____

_____

2 **Read Ashley's description of people in her high school. Then write sentences about the people she knew.**

When I was in high school, I knew some people with unusual hobbies. For example, Mike collected chess pieces – and he didn't even play chess! My best friend, Katrina, loved animals. She went to the zoo every day after school. A girl in my science class painted pictures of insects. Another girl in the same class watched old movies every weekend. Two boys in my English class liked to go hiking in the rain. The basketball coach, Miss Thomas, liked to juggle. My math teacher, Mr. Marks, wrote poetry, and Ms. Spencer, the librarian, made her own clothes. It was an interesting school!

1. *Ashley knew a boy who collected chess pieces.*

2. _____

3. _____

4. _____

5. _____

6. _____

7. _____

8. _____

Lesson 16 — Who's that girl?

1 Complete the conversation with tag questions.

Cristina Hi. You're new at this school, _aren't you_ ?

Anita Yes, I am. You're in my English class, _____?

Cristina Yes, I sit behind you. It's a good class, _____?

Anita Yes, I think so. But the new unit is hard, _____?

Cristina Oh, it's not too bad. Would you like some help?

Anita Sure, that would be great. You're good at English, _____?
Actually, you do well in all your classes, _____?

Cristina No, I don't! I'm terrible at math. But you like math, _____?

Anita Not really. Why do you think so?

Cristina Well, you're carrying your math book, _____?

Anita Yes, I am. We have homework tonight, _____?

Cristina Yes! I forgot!

2 Write tag questions and answers.

1. your cousins / live in the city
   Q: _Your cousins live in the city, don't they?_   **A:** _No, they don't._

2. Louisa / like cats
   Q: _____   **A:** _____

3. Tom / be good at math
   Q: _____   **A:** _____

4. those mountains / be very big
   Q: _____   **A:** _____

5. you / like music
   Q: _____   **A:** _____

6. Diego / play the guitar
   Q: _____   **A:** _____

Get Connected
UNIT 4

1 Read the funny stories quickly. What did the actors star in?

1. _____   2. _____

Famous People - Funny Stories

Hugh Jackman is an Australian actor who played Wolverine in seven different movies, including *The Wolverine* and the *X-Men* movie series. However, he didn't have an easy start.

Just before the first movie, Jackman thought that a wolverine was a wolf. He is a very hardworking person, so he practiced a lot how to act like a wolf. But the director of the X-Men said, "You're a wolverine, not a wolf!". Jackman replied, "But a wolverine isn't a real animal, is it?". "Of course it is." the director answered. "It's a small wild animal, very different from a wolf!". In the end, they both thought that Jackman's mistake was very funny. Harrison Ford is an American actor who starred in the Indiana Jones movies. Ford is usually a friendly and outgoing person who seems to enjoy chatting with people.

He is hardly ever bad-tempered with fans. But sometimes when fans saw him and said, "You're Harrison Ford, aren't you?" he answered, "No, sorry, I'm not Harrison Ford. I just look like him." Recently he decided that this wasn't honest, and he now always answers truthfully. One day, a woman saw him and said, "You look just like Harrison Ford." Ford was honest and said, "Yes, I *am* Harrison Ford." He was surprised — the woman didn't believe him!

2 Complete the sentences with the words in the box.

☐ bad-tempered   ☑ chatting   ☐ forgetful   ☐ just like   ☐ outgoing

1. I like hanging out and _chatting_ with my friends. We always have a lot to talk about.

2. Sorry I can't remember your name. I'm very _____ .

3. Our neighbor is very _____ . He gets angry about everything.

4. My sister is really _____ . She loves meeting new people.

5. You look _____ your mother in her high school photos!

3 Read the stories in Part 1 slowly. Check (✓) the correct words to complete the sentences.

1. Rowan Atkinson is   ☑ a British actor.   ☐ an American actor.

2. At the restaurant Atkinson forgot   ☐ to bring his money.   ☐ to order his food.

3. People in the restaurant thought that Atkinson   ☐ wasn't honest.   ☐ was funny.

4. Harrison Ford is usually   ☐ a bad-tempered person.   ☐ an outgoing person.

5. When Ford answered the woman he   ☐ was honest.   ☐ wasn't honest.

1 **Write tag questions. Use gerunds as subjects or objects. Then write the answers.**

1. Sara / like / dance

   Sara likes dancing, doesn't she? _____ (no) *No, she doesn't.* _____

2. play chess / difficult

   _____ (yes) _____

3. you / enjoy / go to the movies

   _____ (no) _____

4. send e-mail and chat online / popular

   _____ (yes) _____

2 **Look at the pictures. Write sentences with *too* or *either*.**

Lucinda / Joe ①

Tino / Kevin ②

Lola / Tom ③

Marco / Laurel ④

1. (creative) *Lucinda is creative. Joe is, too.* _____

2. (not organized) _____

3. (thoughtful) _____

4. (doesn't always remember things) _____

3 **Look at the information. Then write sentences with *who*.**

Lance Armstrong	David Wright	Jennifer Garner	Jennifer Lopez
cyclist	baseball player	actor	singer
has some children	plays for the New York Mets	likes kickboxing	sings in English and Spanish

1. *Lance Armstrong is a cyclist who has some children.* _____

2. _____

3. _____

4. _____

1 Write the present perfect form of the verb.

1. be _have been_
2. call _____
3. clean _____
4. do _____
5. eat _____

6. go _____
7. hang out _____
8. have _____
9. make _____
10. play _____

11. read _____
12. rent _____
13. see _____
14. study _____
15. watch _____

2 Complete the text with the present perfect.

My best friend and I _____ (do) a lot of fun things this year.
We _____ (watch) six soccer games, we _____ (go)
to 12 movies, and we _____ (hang out) at the beach every weekend.
I _____ (not do) all of my homework, and I _____ (not clean)
my room. My parents aren't happy, but I am!

3 You and your friend are planning a party. Look at your list. Then write
sentences about the things you have done (✓) and the things you
haven't done (✗).

To Do
✗ rent DVDs
✓ invite friends
✓ clean the kitchen
✗ clean the living room
✓ make the decorations
✗ go to the store
✓ make a cake
✗ finish all our chores

1. _We haven't rented DVDs._
2. _____
3. _____
4. _____
5. _____
6. _____
7. _____
8. _____

4 Write about what you have and haven't done.

1. (exercise today) _____
2. (read the newspaper today) _____
3. (watch TV this week) _____
4. (see a movie this week) _____
5. (go to the mountains this year) _____
6. (do my homework today) _____
7. (do chores this week) _____
8. (go shopping this month) _____

UNIT 5 Entertainment

Young entertainers

1 Complete the verb phrases with the words in the box.

☐ entertain ☐ give ☐ record ☐ sign ☑ star ☐ support

1. _____star_____ in a movie
2. _____ interviews
3. _____ a song

4. _____ autographs
5. _____ a charity
6. _____ a live audience

2 What have these entertainers done? What haven't they done? Look at the pictures. Then write sentences with the verb phrases in Part 1.

Ernesto

The Country Girls

1. _Ernesto has supported a charity._
2. _____
3. _____

4. _____
5. _____
6. _____

3 Look at the pictures. Then correct the false information. Use the present perfect.

1. Kaoru / record two CDs

Kaoru hasn't recorded two CDs. She's
recorded three CDs.

2. the Hawks / win soccer games

_____

3. Trevor / appear on TV

_____

4. Isabel / travel to New Zealand

_____

Mini-review

1 Complete the sentences with the present perfect form of the verb phrases in the box.

> ☐ appear in the school newspaper ☑ meet a lot of artists
> ☐ give interviews ☐ record one song
> ☐ have too much homework ☐ not win an Academy Award
> ☐ not make a movie ☐ not win any games

1. I'm a photographer. I go to a lot of parties, and I
   have met a lot of artists .

2. That new singer, Andreas, _____ .
   He wants to record a whole CD next year.

3. The school basketball team has practiced a lot this year,
   but they _____ .

4. My friend wants to be a filmmaker. He
   _____ , but he's edited a movie.

5. They are very popular. They _____
   to every news show on TV!

6. My picture hasn't been in any fashion magazines, but
   it _____ twice.

7. Iliana hasn't had time to hang out this week.
   She _____ .

8. Beyoncé is my favorite singer and actor. She _____ ,
   but she has won many Grammy Awards!

2 Complete the sentences about Cheryl. Use the present perfect. Then write sentences about yourself and people you know.

1. Cheryl _has been_ (be) busy this week.
   I've been busy this week, too. OR _I haven't been busy this week._

2. Cheryl's friends _____ (have) a lot of homework.
   _____

3. She _____ (see) some good TV shows today.
   _____

4. Cheryl's family _____ (not eat) dinner together this week.
   _____

5. She _____ (not go) to the mall this month.
   _____

6. Cheryl _____ (read) the newspaper every day this week.
   _____

Are you a fan?

1 Complete the conversation. Write present perfect questions with *ever*, and answer the questions.

Luciano I'm having trouble with my English composition. We have to write about our lives. But I've had a very boring life!

Jordan No, you haven't! Let's think. (try / any dangerous sports) *Have you ever tried any dangerous sports?*

Luciano (No) *No, I haven't.* I'm not very athletic.

Jordan (meet / movie star) _____

Luciano (No) _____ I'm not interested in movies. I like music.

Jordan OK. (go / any concerts) _____

Luciano (Yes) _____ My friends and I have gone to a few concerts.

Jordan (be invited / backstage) _____

Luciano (Yes) _____ We've been invited backstage a few times. It was fun.

Jordan Wow! (get / any autographs) _____

Luciano (No) _____ But maybe next time!

Jordan Maybe! And you have something to write about now.

2 Answer the questions.

1. **Q:** Have you ever written a fan letter?

   A: *Yes, I have.* I wrote a fan letter to David Beckham.

2. **Q:** Have your friends ever won tickets to a concert?

   A: _____ They never win contests!

3. **Q:** Has your best friend ever helped you with your homework?

   A: _____ He helps me every day.

4. **Q:** Have your friends ever given you presents?

   A: _____ They give me presents for all my birthdays.

5. **Q:** Have you ever tried water-skiing?

   A: _____ I don't like water sports.

6. **Q:** Has your mother ever gone to a concert?

   A: _____ She went to a lot of concerts when she was younger.

3 Answer the questions with your own information.

1. Have you ever been interviewed? _____

2. Has your best friend ever appeared on TV? _____

3. Has your school ever been in the newspaper? _____

4. Has your favorite singer ever won an award? _____

5. Have you ever traveled to another city? _____

6. Have you ever gotten a star's autograph? _____

Lesson 20 Pop culture trivia

1 Write questions and answers.

1. (Keanu Reeves / be an actor) _How long has Keanu Reeves been an actor?_
   (he was in high school) _He's been an actor since he was in high school._

2. (Tiger Woods / play professional golf) _____
   (1996) _____

3. (Kany Garcia / live in Puerto Rico) _____
   (all her life) _____

4. (the Sprouse twins / work as actors) _____
   (more than 16 years) _____

5. (Miley Cyrus / star in *Hannah Montana*) _____
   (2006) _____

6. (the Jonas Brothers / be a rock group) _____
   (more than five years) _____

7. (*Survivor* / be a popular TV show) _____
   (about 2000) _____

8. (Katie Holmes / be married to Tom Cruise) _____
   (2006) _____

2 Look at the chart. Write questions and answers about Elias.

played the guitar – since he was 11
written music – 2010
lived in Los Angeles – 5 years
worked as a musician – 3 years
played in a band – 2013

1. **Q:** _How long has Elias played the guitar?_
   A: _He's played the guitar since he was 11._
2. **Q:** _____
   A: _____
3. **Q:** _____
   A: _____
4. **Q:** _____
   A: _____
5. **Q:** _____
   A: _____

34 Unit 5

Get Connected
UNIT 5

1 **Read the Web site about Dakota Fanning quickly. What does she collect?**

_____

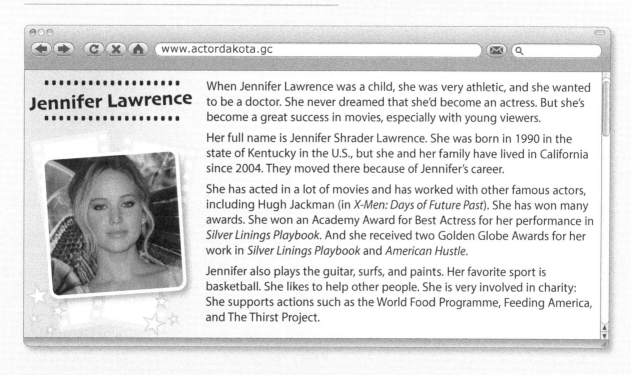

www.actordakota.gc

Jennifer Lawrence

When Jennifer Lawrence was a child, she was very athletic, and she wanted to be a doctor. She never dreamed that she'd become an actress. But she's become a great success in movies, especially with young viewers.

Her full name is Jennifer Shrader Lawrence. She was born in 1990 in the state of Kentucky in the U.S., but she and her family have lived in California since 2004. They moved there because of Jennifer's career.

She has acted in a lot of movies and has worked with other famous actors, including Hugh Jackman (in *X-Men: Days of Future Past*). She has won many awards. She won an Academy Award for Best Actress for her performance in *Silver Linings Playbook*. And she received two Golden Globe Awards for her work in *Silver Linings Playbook* and *American Hustle*.

Jennifer also plays the guitar, surfs, and paints. Her favorite sport is basketball. She likes to help other people. She is very involved in charity: She supports actions such as the World Food Programme, Feeding America, and The Thirst Project.

2 **Complete the sentences with the words in the box.**

☐ career ☑ charity ☐ come true ☐ received ☐ viewers

1. Many stars donate a lot of money to ___*charity*___ .

2. I still haven't _____ the postcard you sent from Hawaii.

3. I hope that all of your dreams _____ .

4. Do you know how many _____ watched the Olympics on TV?

5. I'd like to have a _____ that helps people.

3 **Read the Web site in Part 1 slowly. Answer the questions.**

1. When was Dakota Fanning born? _*She was born in 1994.*_____

2. Where do Dakota and her family live? _____

3. How long have they lived there? _____

4. Has she ever acted in a movie with Tom Cruise? _____

5. What award did she receive for *Charlotte's Web*? _____

6. What does she like to do when she isn't working? _____

1 **Write questions and answers with the present perfect.**

1. A (you / ever meet a sports star) *Have you ever met a sports star?*
   B (no) *No, I haven't.*

2. A (your parents / ever listen to your CDs) _____
   B (yes) _____

3. A (you / be busy / this month) _____
   B (yes) _____

4. A (you / buy any new clothes / this week) _____
   B (no) _____

5. A (Luis and Ramon / ever join a fan club) _____
   B (yes) _____

2 **Dennis and Fernando are musicians. Look at the information. Then write sentences about what they have done (✓) and have not done (✗).**

1. *Dennis has written songs.*
2. _____
3. _____
4. _____
5. _____
6. _____
7. _____
8. _____

DENNIS	FERNANDO
✓ write songs	✓ play the guitar
✗ play the guitar	✓ play at a club
✗ record a song	✗ play with a band
✓ entertain a live audience	✓ win a talent competition

3 **Write questions and answers.**

1. **Q:** (you / be a student at this school) *How long have you been a student at this school?*
   A: (September) *I've been a student at this school since September.*

2. **Q:** (Alicia / live here) _____
   A: (three months) _____

3. **Q:** (your parents / have their car) _____
   A: (a year) _____

4. **Q:** (Tomas and Sarah / be Madonna fans) _____
   A: (1985) _____

5. **Q:** (your brother / speak Portuguese) _____
   A: (two years) _____

6. **Q:** (you / play in a rock band) _____
   A: (2003) _____

Taking risks

1 Make verb phrases with the words below and the verbs in the box.
Then write sentences with the verb phrases and your own information.

☐ dye   ☑ go   ☐ ride   ☐ start
☐ explore   ☐ go out   ☐ sing   ☐ try

1. skydiving _____go skydiving_____ _I've never gone skydiving._
2. my hair _____ _____
3. a band _____ _____
4. a cave _____ _____
5. a motorcycle _____ _____
6. new food _____ _____
7. karaoke _____ _____
8. without permission _____ _____

2 The Medina family has not done any of these things.
Write questions and answers.

1. **Q:** Have Mr. and Mrs. Medina ever been in a
sports competition?

 A: _No, they haven't. They've never been in a sports_
competition. OR _No, never._

2. **Q:** _____

 A: No, they haven't. Darin and Tessa have never
sung karaoke.

3. **Q:** _____

 A: No, she hasn't. Tessa has never gone horseback riding.

4. **Q:** Have the Medinas ever gone hiking in the jungle?

 A: _____

5. **Q:** Has Darin ever acted in a play?

 A: _____

6. **Q:** Has Max ever gone camping with the family?

 A: _____

Lesson 22 — What we've done

1 Complete the sentences with *ago, for, since,* or *so far.*

1. I've liked classical music *for* many years.

2. She hasn't read comic books _____ she was a child.

3. Our volleyball team has done really well _____ .

4. I've studied English _____ five years.

5. Enrique met his new teacher a week _____ .

6. Carlo hasn't scored a goal in this game _____ .

7. I went to Puerto Rico with my family two months _____ .

8. I haven't gotten any e-mail messages _____ Friday.

2 Complete the conversation with the simple past or the present perfect.

Josh Hi, Emily. Where *have you been* (you / be)? _____ (I / not see) you for a long time.

Emily I know. _____ (I / be) in Dallas with my cousins. _____ (I / come back) a week ago.

Josh What _____ (you / do) there?

Emily _____ (I / go) horseback riding every day. _____ (My cousins / have) their own horses since _____ (they / be) young kids.

Josh Do you like horseback riding? Did you fall off the horse?

Emily I love it, and _____ (I / not fall off) at all! Actually, I think horseback riding is the best thing _____ (I / do) so far this year.

3 Answer the questions with your own information.

1. What's something you've done since you were a small child?

   _____

2. What did you do last weekend?

   _____

3. What have you done since last summer?

   _____

4. What holiday or event has your family celebrated for many years?

   _____

5. What's the most interesting thing you've learned so far this year?

   _____

Mini-review

1 Choose the correct word to complete the sentences.

1. Have you _ever_ (ever / never) tried Indian food?

2. Two of my friends _____ (have gone / went) skydiving last week.

3. I've had a lot of interesting experiences _____ (for / since) last year.

4. My father ran a marathon two months _____ (ago / since).

5. _____ (Did you have / Have you had) a good time yesterday?

6. Cindy has _____ (ever / never) played with a rock band.

7. Ken hasn't won any prizes _____ (since / so far).

8. I haven't seen my best friend _____ (for / since) two weeks.

2 Look at the information. Then write questions and long answers about Christina.

Christina

1. sail a boat → two weeks ago

2. meet a rock star → never

3. have a pet → since she was five

4. be a recreation leader → for a long time

5. run a marathon → last year

6. write e-mail messages in English → never

1. **Q:** _Has Christina ever sailed a boat?_
   A: _Yes, she has. She sailed a boat two weeks ago._

2. **Q:** _____
   A: _____

3. **Q:** _____
   A: _____

4. **Q:** _____
   A: _____

5. **Q:** _____
   A: _____

6. **Q:** _____
   A: _____

Amazing teens

1 **Fidel and Paco are traveling around Australia. Write sentences about what they have already done and what they have not done yet.**

1. _They've already hiked in the rain forest._

2. _____

3. _____

4. _____

5. _____

6. _____

7. _____

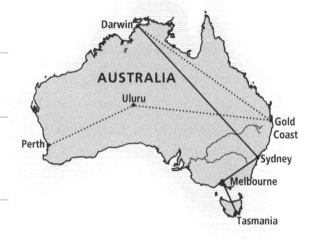

THINGS TO DO IN AUSTRALIA

☑ Tasmania: hike in rain forest

☑ Melbourne: go to a rock concert

☑ Sydney: see the Sydney Opera House

☐ the Gold Coast: go scuba diving

☑ Darwin: tour the crocodile farm

☐ Uluru: climb the rock

☐ Perth: try surfing

2 **Correct the false statements about Fidel and Paco.**

1. Paco hasn't been to Tasmania yet.

   He's already been to Tasmania.

2. Fidel and Paco have already visited Perth.

   _____

3. Fidel and Paco have already visited the Gold Coast.

   _____

4. Fidel hasn't been to Darwin yet.

   _____

5. Paco and Fidel haven't been to Melbourne yet.

   _____

6. Fidel has already tried surfing.

   _____

7. Fidel and Paco have already been to Uluru.

   _____

8. Paco hasn't seen the Sydney Opera House yet.

   _____

Lesson 24 In the spotlight

1 Complete the conversation with tag questions.

Mrs. Nelson	Hello. You're in my math class this year, _____aren't you_____ ?
Curtis	Uh, no, I'm not. I'm in Mrs. Smith's class.
Mrs. Nelson	Really? But you took her class two years ago, _____ ?
Curtis	No, I didn't.
Mrs. Nelson	But she's taught tenth-grade math for a long time, _____ ?
Curtis	Yes, she has. But I've never taken her class before.
Mrs. Nelson	But you've been a student here since sixth grade, _____ ?
Curtis	Yes, I have . . .
Mrs. Nelson	And you've finished ninth grade, _____ ?
Curtis	Yes, I have. I'm in tenth grade now.
Mrs. Nelson	Wait a minute. Are you Chris Wilson?
Curtis	No, I'm not. I'm his younger brother, Curtis!
Mrs. Nelson	Oh. I'm sorry. Then Chris is in my class, and so is your cousin, Emma. They've always been good at math, _____ ?

2 Write tag questions. Then answer them with your own information.

1. you / be a student / at this school / three years

   Q: _You've been a student at this school for three years,_   **A:** _Yes, I have._

   haven't you?

2. last summer / be very hot

   Q: _____   **A:** _____

3. you / pass sixth-grade math

   Q: _____   **A:** _____

4. your classmates / always be / good students

   Q: _____   **A:** _____

5. soccer / be a popular sport in your country / long time

   Q: _____   **A:** _____

6. your friends / live in this town / they were born

   Q: _____   **A:** _____

7. you / speak English / five years

   Q: _____   **A:** _____

8. your English teacher / give a lot of homework / yesterday

   Q: _____   **A:** _____

1 Read the Web site quickly. What's in a letterbox?

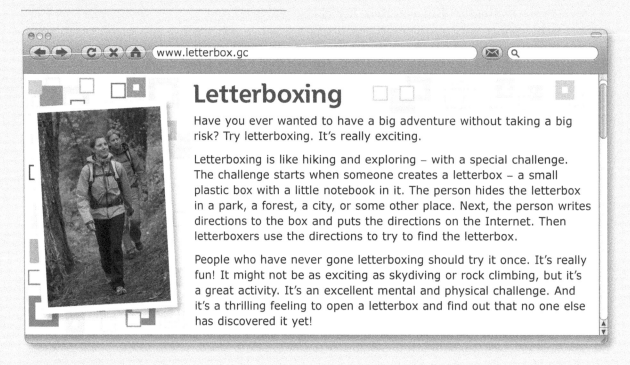

www.letterbox.gc

Letterboxing

Have you ever wanted to have a big adventure without taking a big risk? Try letterboxing. It's really exciting.

Letterboxing is like hiking and exploring – with a special challenge. The challenge starts when someone creates a letterbox – a small plastic box with a little notebook in it. The person hides the letterbox in a park, a forest, a city, or some other place. Next, the person writes directions to the box and puts the directions on the Internet. Then letterboxers use the directions to try to find the letterbox.

People who have never gone letterboxing should try it once. It's really fun! It might not be as exciting as skydiving or rock climbing, but it's a great activity. It's an excellent mental and physical challenge. And it's a thrilling feeling to open a letterbox and find out that no one else has discovered it yet!

2 Complete the sentences with the words in the box.

☐ hides   ☐ mental   ☐ risk   ☑ rock climbing   ☐ skydiving

1. We did some _rock climbing_ when we took a vacation in the mountains.

2. I don't want to go _____ because I'm afraid of flying.

3. My father always _____ our birthday presents, and we have to find them.

4. Stress isn't good for your body, and it's not good for your _____ health, either.

5. I don't think it's a good idea to take a _____ with your safety.

3 Read the Web site in Part 1 slowly. Circle the correct words to complete the sentences.

1. Letterboxing is ((an exciting)/ a risky) activity.

2. When people go letterboxing, they are also (hiking / rock climbing).

3. In this article, a letterbox is (a place to mail a letter / a little plastic box).

4. You can find directions to letterboxes (in the forest / on the Internet).

5. People who have never gone letterboxing (should never do it / should do it once).

6. When someone opens a letterbox (many people have / no one has) discovered it yet.

1 **Choose the correct words to complete the sentences.**

1. I studied art _____*for*_____ (for / since) two weeks last summer.
2. Our last concert was two months _____ (since / ago).
3. They've _____ (already / yet) finished their science projects.
4. I haven't gone shopping _____ (so far / since) last weekend.
5. We haven't found summer jobs _____ (already / yet).
6. Laura has done very well in class _____ (so far / ago).
7. I've learned a lot of new English words _____ (ago / so far) this year.
8. Danny has _____ (yet / already) cleaned his room.

2 **Complete the interview with tag questions and answers.**

Reporter Hello, Charlie. I'm going to ask you some questions. _____*You've been*_____ (you / be) a violinist since you were about six years old, _____*haven't you*_____ ?

Charlie Yes, _____ .

Reporter Your parents _____ (buy) you your first violin a long time ago, _____ ?

Charlie No, _____ . My brother bought it for me. He's a great brother.

Reporter _____ (you / entertain a live audience) for the first time when you were 11, _____ ?

Charlie Yes, _____ . I was very proud!

Reporter And since then, _____ (you / play) in many countries, _____ ?

Charlie No, _____ . I've never performed outside the U.S.!

3 **Write present perfect questions with *ever*. Then write answers with *never*.**

1. **Q:** (you / travel to England) _*Have you ever traveled to England?*_
   A: _*No, I haven't. I've never traveled to England.*_ OR _*No, never.*_
2. **Q:** (Maria / go to a rain forest) _____
   A: _____
3. **Q:** (you / dye your hair) _____
   A: _____
4. **Q:** (John / try rock climbing) _____
   A: _____
5. **Q:** (Jen and Ron / win a marathon) _____
   A: _____
6. **Q:** (Martina / meet a famous person) _____
   A: _____

Teen opinions

1 Complete the sentences with the correct forms of the adjectives.

1. *Iron Man* was ___the best___ (good) movie of the year!
2. My mother's cookies are _____ (good) your mother's cookies.
3. _____ (bad) show on TV is *Tough Times*. I don't like it at all.
4. Mary Ann is a _____ (good) friend. She always talks to me when I feel sad.
5. I don't like watching sports very much. I think watching basketball games is _____ (bad) watching tennis matches. Basketball is so boring.
6. It's a _____ (good) song. I really love it!
7. I don't like this food. It tastes pretty _____ (bad).
8. I think Saturday is _____ (good) day of the week. I can sleep late on Saturdays!

2 Write sentences with the comparative or superlative form of the adjectives.

1. *The Adventures of Huckleberry Finn* / good / book in the library
   Superlative: *The Adventures of Huckleberry Finn is the best book in the library.*
2. your grades / good / my grades
   Comparative: _____
3. Gregorio's Restaurant / have / bad pizza in town
   Superlative: _____
4. this band / play / good music / that band
   Comparative: _____
5. P.E. / bad / math
   Comparative: _____
6. Monday / bad / day of the week
   Superlative: _____
7. cats / good / dogs
   Comparative: _____
8. soccer / good / sport to play
   Superlative: _____

3 Write sentences with the adjectives and your own information.

1. (messy) *My room is always messy.* _____
2. (beautiful) _____
3. (entertaining) _____
4. (awful) _____
5. (difficult) _____
6. (scary) _____

Unforgettable moments

1 **Write the superlative form of the adjectives.**

1. disgusting *the most disgusting*
2. thrilling _____
3. difficult _____
4. beautiful _____
5. happy _____

6. short _____
7. funny _____
8. exciting _____
9. young _____
10. unforgettable _____

2 **Answer the questions. Use the superlative +** *have ever.*

1. **A** Is the movie good?

   B Yes, (movie / see) *it is. It's the best movie I've ever seen* .

2. **A** Is the book you're reading scary?

   B Yes, (book / read) _____ .

3. **A** Is your cousin forgetful?

   B Yes, (person / meet) _____ .

4. **A** Is the homework assignment frustrating?

   B Yes, (assignment / do) _____ .

5. **A** Is your brother's room messy?

   B Yes, (room / see) _____ .

6. **A** Are your classes interesting?

   B Yes, (classes / take) _____ .

7. **A** Is the food at that restaurant bad?

   B Yes, (food / eat) _____ .

8. **A** Is your family's new car big?

   B Yes, (car / have) _____ .

3 **Answer the questions with your own information.**

1. Who's the tallest person you've ever met?

   My uncle is the tallest person I've ever met.

2. What's the longest book you've ever read?

   _____

3. What's the scariest movie you've ever seen?

   _____

4. What's the hardest class you've ever taken?

   _____

5. Who's the funniest person you've ever met?

   _____

6. What's the most delicious food you've ever eaten?

   _____

1 **What are these people saying? Look at the pictures, and write sentences.**

1. (desk / messy) *Your desk is very messy.*
   It's messier than my desk. It's the
   messiest desk I've ever seen.

2. (bicycle / nice) _____
   _____

3. (pet / scary) _____
   _____
   _____

4. (printer / fast) _____
   _____
   _____

2 **Look at Damon's list. Then write sentences using the superlative + *have ever*.**

1. (sport / try) *Skiing is the most difficult sport he's ever tried.*

2. (movie / see) _____

3. (book / read) _____

4. (person / meet) _____

5. (CD / buy) _____

6. (place / visit) _____

difficult sport — skiing
funny movie — *School Vacation*
bad book — *The Long Road*
interesting person — Professor Alden
good CD — *The Greatest Hits*
                Collection by Alan Jackson
beautiful place — Ipanema Beach

Are we alike?

1 **Write sentences comparing the people and the items.**

1

Don / Dora / tall / short

1. *Don isn't as tall as Dora.*

   Dora isn't as short as Don.

2

black skirt / white skirt / expensive

2. _____

   _____

3

small car / big car / fast / slow

3. _____

   _____

4

Tina / Gina / sad / happy

4. _____

   _____

2 **Read about Ramona's family. Then write sentences using formal comparisons for numbers 1–4 and informal comparisons with object pronouns for numbers 5–8.**

I have a twin brother, Ricardo. We look alike: I'm as tall as him, and I'm as athletic as him. Of course, I'm as old as him! Our personalities are similar, too. We're both artistic, but I'm not as artistic as Ricardo. He isn't as outgoing as me. But we're both very funny. We have two younger sisters. They're cute, but they aren't as funny as us! They're really shy. We're not as shy as them.

1. (Ramona / tall / Ricardo) *Ramona is as tall as he is.*

2. (Ramona / athletic / Ricardo) _____

3. (Ramona / artistic / Ricardo) _____

4. (their sisters / old / Ricardo and Ramona) _____

5. (Ricardo / outgoing / Ramona) *Ricardo isn't as outgoing as her.*

6. (Ramona / funny / Ricardo) _____

7. (Ramona / old / Ricardo) _____

8. (Ramona and Ricardo / shy / their sisters) _____

I'd rather ...

1 **Look at the pictures. Then write sentences with *would rather*.**

1. (Lucia / take piano lessons / dance lessons) *Lucia would rather take dance lessons*
   than piano lessons.

2. (Pete and Rick / read books / watch TV) _____

3. (Justin / play soccer / play chess) _____

4. (Katie / eat fruit / eat ice cream) _____

5. (Linda / meet a movie star / meet a sports star) _____

6. (Paul / stay home / go out) _____

2 **Write questions with the verb phrases in the box. Then answer them with your own information.**

> ☐ be funny / be artistic   ☑ buy a radio / buy an MP3 player
> ☐ be tall / be short   ☐ explore an old house / explore a cave

1. **Q:** *Would you rather buy a radio or an MP3 player?*
   A: *I'd rather buy an MP3 player.*

2. **Q:** _____
   A: _____

3. **Q:** _____
   A: _____

4. **Q:** _____
   A: _____

1 Read the article quickly. Who has a job? Check (✓) the correct answer(s).

☐ Carlos ☐ Sherry ☐ Katie

Lazy teens? No way!

Are teens today lazier than teens in past generations? No way! Between school, homework, chores, and part-time jobs the average teen works over 50 hours a week. Read what these hardworking teens say about jobs and their busy lives.

Carlos Fuentes, 17: I really like my job. I'd rather work than hang out at home or the mall. Working is the best way to learn job skills. And I like the money. I'm saving for college because the college I want to go to is the most expensive college in my city.

Sherry Nelson, 16: My parents think I'm too young to have a part-time job. They think a job isn't as important as school. They say the most important thing is studying and getting good grades, and I agree. I play sports after school and do a lot of chores at home, so I really don't have time for a job.

Katie Wu, 17: Doing community work as a volunteer can give you valuable and memorable experiences. When I'm at work, I meet a lot of different people and I have to use my time well. Work isn't as difficult as school, and I like them both.

2 Complete the sentences with the words in the box.

☐ community work ☐ generation ☐ job skills ☐ memorable ☑ valuable

1. Money and success are great, but nothing is more ___valuable___ than your health.

2. Don't expect to find work if you don't have any _____ .

3. People of all ages helped with _____ in our neighborhood last year.

4. You can have _____ experiences as a volunteer.

5. John's grandparents try hard to understand people in John's _____ .

3 Read the article in Part 1 slowly. Match the people with the opinions. Write *C* (Carlos), *S* (Sherry), or *K* (Katie).

1. When I'm at work, I have to use my time well. __K__

2. A job isn't as important for teens as school and other activities. _____

3. Working is a better way to spend free time than hanging out at home. _____

4. I really don't have time for a job. _____

5. Volunteer work gives teens valuable experiences. _____

6. Working is a good way to get money for your education. _____

Unit 7 Check Yourself

1 Write questions and answers.

1. have a cat / have a dog
   Q: *Would you rather have a cat or a dog?*
   A: (cat / cute) *I'd rather have a cat than a dog. Cats are cuter than dogs.*

2. study German / study Italian
   Q: _____
   A: (Italian / not difficult) _____

3. watch *The Dark Cave* / watch *Spider-Man*
   Q: _____
   A: (*Spider-Man* / not scary) _____

4. eat at Bono's Burgers / eat at the Golden Palace
   Q: _____
   A: (the Golden Palace / better food) _____

2 Look at the information. Compare the items using formal and informal comparisons.

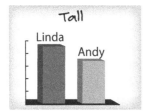

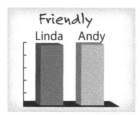
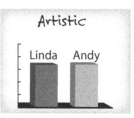

1. (Andy / tall) *Andy isn't as tall as she is.   Andy isn't as tall as her.*
2. (Linda / active) _____
3. (Andy / friendly) _____
4. (Linda / artistic) _____

3 Complete the text with the superlative forms of the words + *have ever*.

If you want to go on a great vacation, go to the Rolling River Ranch. It's
the best place I've ever visited (good place / visit)! I went horseback riding for the
first time there. Horseback riding is _____ (hard sport / try),
but I liked it. The horses there were _____ (big horses / see).
I only fell off once – when I saw a cute boy. That's _____
(embarrassing experience / have). But it was OK. He didn't laugh, and we became
friends. He's _____ (nice boy / meet). Too bad he doesn't live
in my town! But he sends me _____ (long e-mails / read).
Maybe I'll see him again when I go back to the ranch next year.

Our dreams

1 Write sentences.

1. Maria / take a trip next summer / Belize

   If Maria could take a trip next summer, she'd take a trip to Belize.

2. Luis and Renaldo / watch any movie / that new comedy

   _____

3. Marissa and Eliot / join a new club / the photography club

   _____

4. Gisela / buy new clothes / a black dress

   _____

5. my sister / learn a new sport / snowboarding

   _____

6. we / be good at any activity / painting

   _____

7. we / live in any city / San Juan

   _____

8. Jessica and Aileen / have any kind of dessert / chocolate cake

   _____

2 Complete the sentences.

1. _If I could visit any country_, I'd visit Japan.
2. _____, I'd try bowling.
3. _____, I'd talk to Barack Obama.
4. _____, I'd get a dog.
5. _____, I'd look like my favorite star.
6. _____, I'd be good at tennis.
7. _____, I'd buy the new Jonas Brothers CD.

3 Look at Part 2. Rewrite the sentences with your own information.

1. _If I could visit any country, I'd visit Italy._
2. _____
3. _____
4. _____
5. _____
6. _____
7. _____

What would you do?

1 Complete the sentences.

1. If Carrie won a lot of money, _she'd give_____ (give) it to charity.

2. What _____ (you / do) if you found a lost dog?

3. If you broke your promise, _____ (I / be) very angry.

4. What _____ (Lana / do) if she _____ (not pass) her test?

5. If I _____ (lose) this camera, I _____ (not buy) a new one.

2 Complete the sentences with the sentences in the box.

☐ I'd lend it to him   ☐ I'd take it to the Lost and Found
☑ I'd put the garbage in the trash can   ☐ I wouldn't litter. I'd throw it in the trash can

1. If I saw someone litter, _I'd put the garbage in the trash can_____ .

2. If I found an expensive bracelet in the school bathroom, _____ .

3. If I had some garbage, _____ .

4. If my friend needed to borrow some money, _____ .

3 Write questions. Then match the questions to the answers.

1. your friend / ask you to trespass
   What would you do if your friend
   _asked you to trespass?_____ e_

2. your friend / want to gossip
   _____
   _____

3. your sister / break a promise to you
   _____
   _____

4. your friend / lie to you
   _____
   _____

5. you see someone / eavesdropping on
   your conversation
   _____
   _____

6. your brother / cross in the middle of the street
   _____
   _____

a. I'd be angry. Breaking promises
   is really awful.

b. I'd tell him to gossip with
   someone else.

c. I'd move to another place to talk.

d. I'd say, "Jaywalking isn't good.
   You could get hit by a car."

e. I'd refuse. Trespassing is
   dangerous.

f. I'd say, "That isn't true."

Mini-review

1 Write sentences with *if* clauses and *could.*

1. he / go / moon

   If he could go anyplace, he'd go to the moon.

2. Carolyn / meet / Bradley Cooper

3. Andy and Ann / buy / a boat

4. Romeo / live / on an island

2 Write questions. Then answer the questions with your own information.

1. you / find an expensive ring

   Q: *What would you do if you found an expensive ring?*

   A: *If I found an expensive ring, I'd try to find the owner.*

2. you / lose your English book

   Q:

   A:

3. your friend / ask you for some money

   Q:

   A:

4. your brother / lie to you

   Q:

   A:

5. you / fail a test

   Q:

   A:

6. you / meet a famous person

   Q:

   A:

What I'm going to be

1 Circle the two jobs that best match each description.

1. A person who asks many questions ⬭detective⬭   carpenter   ⬭scientist⬭
2. A person who flies in a vehicle   astronaut   pilot   computer programmer
3. A person who likes adventure   detective   veterinarian astronaut
4. A person who makes things   astronaut   artist   carpenter
5. A person who writes a lot   journalist   author   astronaut

2 Write sentences with infinitives to give a reason.

1. I want to make furniture.

   (carpenter) *I want to be a carpenter to make furniture.*

2. Michael wants to paint pictures.

   (artist) _____

3. Carlita is going to work with animals.

   (veterinarian) _____

4. Clara is going to work with children.

   (teacher) _____

5. Will is going to teach martial arts.

   (karate instructor) _____

6. Sarah and Jocelyn would like to travel to outer space.

   (astronauts) _____

7. Carmen is going to write funny stories for children.

   (author) _____

8. My best friend and I want to work with the latest technology.

   (computer programmers) _____

3 Answer the questions with the verb phrases in the box.

> ☐ make discoveries   ☐ star in movies
> ☑ report on events and write articles   ☐ travel to interesting places
> ☐ solve mysteries   ☐ write stories

1. Why are you going to be a journalist? *I'm going to be a journalist to report on events and write articles.*

2. Why is Carol going to be a detective? _____

3. Why does your sister want to be a pilot? _____

4. Why would Hector like to be an actor? _____

5. Why are you and Amelia going to be authors? _____

6. Why do Camille and Chloe want to be scientists? _____

The past year

1 **Choose the correct words to complete the sentences.**

1. I can't think of _anything_ (anything / something) to do today.
2. My uncle is _____ (anyone / someone) I admire.
3. I haven't met _____ (anyone / someone) famous.
4. I don't want to go _____ (anywhere / somewhere) this weekend.
5. Tom went _____ (anywhere / somewhere) really cool last weekend.
6. My teacher said _____ (anything / something) that I don't understand.

2 **Complete the conversation with *anyone, anything, anywhere, someone, something,* or *somewhere.***

Melinda Hi, Gloria. What are you doing here?

Gloria I'm looking for a birthday present for ___*someone*___ .

Melinda Oh? Is the present for _____ I know?

Gloria Well, . . . it's for Brad, my boyfriend.

Melinda I see! It's for _____ special. What are you going to buy?

Gloria I don't know! I can't think of _____ he likes.

Melinda He likes baseball, doesn't he? Buy him _____ he can use when he plays baseball. How about a glove?

Gloria A glove? I can't buy him _____ like that! That's too weird.

Melinda OK. Then buy him a gift certificate for a restaurant. Then he can take you _____ nice.

Gloria Good idea! Can you think of _____ I can buy one?

3 **Write questions. Then answer them with your own information.**

1. meet someone special / this year

   Q: _Have you met anyone special this year?_   **A:** _Yes, I met someone at the beach._

   OR _No, I haven't met anyone special this year._

2. go somewhere new / last week

   Q: _____   **A:** _____

3. have / do something fun / this month

   Q: _____   **A:** _____

4. there is something new / on TV / tonight

   Q: _____   **A:** _____

5. give someone a present / last month

   Q: _____   **A:** _____

6. eat somewhere special / last month

   Q: _____   **A:** _____

Get Connected
UNIT 8

1 Read the Web site quickly. Whose idea do you think is best? _____

Help Fight World Hunger

What would you do if you wanted to help hungry people in the world but you didn't have billions of dollars? We asked some students for their ideas.

Timothy: If a friend would join me, I'd volunteer with an organization or foundation that works to fight world hunger. Maybe we could travel to another country to help people. It would be a good education about other countries for us, too.

Gwen: I would get photographs of children who don't have enough to eat. I would put the photos on a Web site with this question: *What would you do if these children were yours?* I would also list the names of organizations that help fight world hunger. Then I would send the link for the Web site to people and ask them to donate money to help hungry children.

Ray: I'd write a letter to a celebrity. In the letter, I'd ask the celebrity to come and talk at our school. I'd ask all of the students in our school to sign the letter. People would pay money to go to the talk, and we would use the money to help fight hunger.

These are great ideas – but send us yours! What could you do to help hungry people?

2 Complete the sentences with the words in the box.

☐ billions ☑ celebrity ☐ donate ☐ education ☐ foundations

1. My favorite ___celebrity___ does a lot of work for charity.

2. A lot of money for charities comes from big _____ .

3. When you get a new computer, _____ your old one to a charity.

4. The Internet isn't just for entertainment. It also helps with _____ .

5. I think countries should stop spending _____ of dollars to fight with each other.

3 Read the Web site in Part 1 slowly. Write the name of the correct student or students.

1. ___Timothy___ would travel to another country.

2. _____ would ask someone to come to the school and talk.

3. _____ would use photographs.

4. _____ would ask people to pay money to attend an event.

5. _____ would volunteer.

6. _____ and _____ want to raise money.

1 What are Missy's dreams? Write sentences.

1. travel to any country
   If Missy could travel to any country, she'd travel to Brazil.

2. get any gift
   _____

3. meet any movie star
   _____

4. study any subject
   _____

My Dreams
.travel to Brazil .meet Angelina Jolie
.get a DVD player .study computer science

2 Write sentences about Missy's reasons for her choices. Use the information from Part 1 and the verb phrases in the box.

☐ get an autograph   ☐ learn to design Web sites   ☑ see the rain forest   ☐ watch movies

1. *She's going to travel to Brazil to see the rain forest.* _____
2. _____
3. _____
4. _____

3 Complete the sentences with *anyone, anything, anywhere, someone, something,* or *somewhere*.

1. Did you do ____*anything*____ special last weekend?
2. I'm going to meet _____ special tonight – my girlfriend.
3. I did _____ interesting this month. I built my own computer!
4. I can't think of _____ else to invite to my party.
5. I want to go _____ warm this winter.
6. They didn't go _____ last summer.

4 Complete the questions and answers with the correct conditional form of the verbs.

1. **Q:** What *would you do* (you / do) *if you won* (you / win) a lot of money?

   A: *If I won a lot of money, I'd take a trip* (take a trip) somewhere.

2. **Q:** What _____ (your parents / do) _____ (you / stay out late)?

   A: _____ (they / be) angry.

3. **Q:** What _____ (your sister / do) _____ (you / go) into her room without permission?

   A: _____ (she / tell) my parents.

Illustration Credits

Adolar 8, 47, 57

Paulo Borges 4, 9, 25, 37, 48

Chuck Gonzales 2, 15, 26, 32, 40, 53

Adam Hurwitz 38, 40

Marcelo Pacheco 17, 24, 29, 46

Terry Wong 5, 20, 31, 45

Photo Acknowledgements

The authors and publishers acknowledge the following sources of copyright material and are grateful for the permissions granted. While every effort has been made, it has not always been possible to identify the sources of all the material used, or to trace all copyright holders. If any omissions are brought to our notice, we will be happy to include the appropriate acknowledgements on reprinting.

Workbook

p. 3: ©Howard Grey/The Image Bank/Getty Images; p. 6: ©Rob Marmion/Shutterstock; p. 7 (L): ©Eugene Sergeev/ Shutterstock; p. 7 (R): ©Dianne Avery Photography/Moment/Getty Images; p. 10: ©Brand X Pictures/Stockbyte/ Getty Images Plus/Getty Images; p. 11: ©Brand X Pictures/Stockbyte/Getty Images Plus/Getty Images; p. 13 (L): ©Digital Vision/Photodisc/Getty Images; p. 13 (R): ©Ryan McVay/Photodisc/Getty Images; p. 14: ©Art on File/ Corbis; p. 16: ©Alfaguarilla/Shutterstock; p. 18 (T): ©Commercial Eye/The Image Bank/Getty Images; p. 18 (B): ©Bounce/Cultura/Getty Images; p. 19: ©Ben Blankenburg/Corbis; p. 21: ©SW Productions/Photodisc/Getty Images; p. 22: ©Ben Blankenburg/Corbis; p. 23: ©altrendo images/Stockbyte/Getty Images; p. 25: ©Image Source/Alamy; p. 27 (TL): ©Juice Images/Corbis; p. 27 (TC): ©237/Robert Daly/Ocean/Corbis; p. 27 (TR): ©Jose Luis Pelaez Inc/ Blend Images/Getty Images; p. 27 (BL): ©incamerastock/Alamy; p. 27 (BC): ©Sean Justice/Photodisc/Getty Images; p. 27 (BR): ©Ron Levine/Taxi/Getty Images; p. 28 (L): ©D Dipasupil/FilmMagic; p. 28 (R): ©Jason LaVeris/ FilmMagic/Getty Images; p. 30: ©Jacek Chabraszewski/Shutterstock; p. 33: ©I Love Images/Corbis; p. 34: ©g-stockstudio/Shutterstock; p. 35: ©Startraks Photo/REX Shutterstock; p. 39: ©Onne van der Wal/Corbis; p. 40: ©Sergio Pitamitz/Alamy; p. 42: ©Scott Markewitz/Photographer's Choice/Getty Images; p. 43: ©Hill Street Studios/ Blend Images/Getty Images; p. 44 (T): ©Nancy Honey/The Image Bank/Getty Images; p. 44 (B): ©Greg Ceo/Taxi/ Getty Images; p. 48: ©Gage/The Image Bank/Getty Images; p. 49: ©Juan Silva/The Image Bank/Getty Images; p. 51 (T): ©Photoshot Holdings Ltd/Alamy; p. 51 (B): ©Sean Pavone/Shutterstock; p. 53 (L): ©Arthur Morris/CORBIS; p. 53 (CL): ©Jason Merritt/Getty Images; p. 53 (CR): ©Elena Elisseeva/Shutterstock; p. 53 (R): ©Ian Bracegirdle/ Shutterstock; p. 54: ©John Lund/Marc Romanelli/Blend Images/Getty Images; p. 55: ©Chris Windsor/Photodisc/ Getty Images; p. 56: ©PATRICK BARTH/REX Shutterstock.

Cover photograph by ©Siberia - Video and Photo/Shutterstock.

Notes

Notes

Notes

Notes